I ♥ YOU MOM

Mom Coloring Book

GINA TROWLER

Our love
is shared
in a thousand
different
ways...

ISBN-13: 978-1522983064

MOM COLORING TIPS

1. Find a quiet place to do your coloring.

2. Choose your colors according to your liking. Be light and open-minded.

3. Choose to color in bright natural light whenever possible.

4. Make sure you are sitting in a comfortable seat with good back support. Relax.

5. Don't be afraid to express your creativity and imagination in your coloring.

6. Pick your favorite artwork patterns to color.

7. Color at a time when you are least likely to be interrupted.

8. If you like classical music, switch it on and play it softly in the background.

9. Choose coloring pencils over regular crayons to do your coloring

10. If you like to use art markers, it is best to use a sheet of craft plastic under the coloring page.

11. Stop coloring whenever you feel like stopping.

12. Whatever the outcome, it is your own expression and masterpiece.

IMPORTANT:

In order to prevent color-bleeding no images were placed on the opposite side of each artwork printed.

Mom, I love you to the moon and back!

Made in the USA
Middletown, DE
05 May 2016